THE
LOST
ARABS

THE LOST ARABS

OMAR SAKR

Andrews McMeel
PUBLISHING®

For Candy Royalle,
gone too soon but never lost

&

my brother, Mohomad,
without whom I could not do what I do

Here We Are

People don't seem to understand.
They say no, look, hell is over where the grass is
greener. Or no, look, it's where blood drenches
everything. Nobody wants to reckon with
the truth of this place. A palace in hell is still
in hell. Freedom of movement in hell is still—listen,
hell is any place where someone is being tortured
and we have been here for the longest time.

Contents

THE
LOST
ARABS

Boys with Their Pins Pulled

Call it what you will, this place,
like everywhere else beneath the sun,
burns. The boys spread through it
like fuel before the fire, torn khakis
muted in the dust kicked up by the fuss.
They are yelling or the earth is,
and the noise is flame.

           The residents
always leave a residue. A spreading
stain, like these boys, if boys they are.
Everything has a name. Some are erased,
others misplaced, gifted and taken
away, or replaced. Here we have
little stacks of mapped bone,
they are kicking a ball while the men
search what used to be homes.

               Shins
bruised, knees creaking, little bronze
busts gleaming, the ball bounces, if
ball it really is. Rejoice regardless,
someone is scoring a goal, though
the posts are always shifting and
so are the players, both the living
and the dead. Neither is winning,
despite the din,

         the hammerblows
of this forge, making both boys
and grenades indistinguishable.
People scream—look out, duck,

and any thing might be sailing in
the air, a body or a ball or a blast.
Everything loses its form in the end.
A child, frenzied, falls. The others
surround him, a furious sandstorm.
In this nothing space,

                           you never know
what you'll be bending to recover,
whether your fingers will meet skin,
plastic, or metal. No matter, the result
is always the same: a name erupting.

As the Bombed City Swells
(in a Viral Video)

And the streets become rivers of no
longer rushing water, wide and flat,
dark and calm, a wending mirror
of sky snakes its way between
each small building of mud brick
and stone. A man drifts
                              on a door
of a home or sheet of unclear metal,
his handmade keffiyeh chequered red
and white around his dusty head, a pole
in hand to convince the river to yield
in the only tongue it knows: urgency,
rhythmic and insistent, a language
of push pull give take.
                              Laughing, the man
and his new canoe explore the reborn
city, a desert wetness, even as others wade
through the hip-high liquid roads, collecting
debris, bemoaning the fate that scattered
pots and pans, children and names,
a past always floating just out of reach.
When will the burst dam be fixed, they say,
or is this the ocean's angry work?
                              Fools,
the rootless man replies, look to the future—
do you not see the oasis has come to us,
do you not see me blooming here
like the rarest of flowers? Truly, the Arab
Spring has arrived.

Hanging Dry in Athens

Who set the sky on fire? all the children
ask, pointing little grubby fingers like guns
at the sculpted grey banks backlit by flame
or at least a sullen orange glare

as if a giant tulip is budding there
but when told so, none of them are fooled.
All their lives paper clouds have resisted
the sun, only now they appear to have caught on.

A hideous wind is brewing, carrying on it
the mewling of men, the acrid tang of teargas
and the first drifting motes of ash. Black snow!
Black snow! the younger boys cry, stomping

about with glee, momentarily forgetting
the ominous horizon glowering in the distance.
Later, from the safety of the hotel, I witness
the caramello sky unwrapping itself in a hurry

as a woman on a nearby rooftop gathers
laundry off a clothesline, her dress and hair
snatched and torn at, unpicking underwear,
then shorts, shirts, jackets, and skirts,

folding them all into a basket as if unaware
an arsonist has set everything ablaze or else,
at the very least, entirely unconcerned
by the ease with which we burn.

House of Beirut
for Mona El Hallak

Once, my ancestors would have been united—in name if nothing else—knighted by the conqueror's blade as Ottoman. Not Lebanese, not Turkish. I cannot imagine the ease of being only one thing. I am sure this too is a fantasy. In Beirut, a memorial is taking over a house where every bullet hole has been given a name, a shrine to the violence that (r)ejected my family. Only in light of this can you call it *Paris*, otherwise leave that imperial shade alone. They say people are afraid to speak of the civil war lest it spark back to life. The war is not taught. Who knew my family have followed official policy for years? They will be devastated to hear it. All my knowledge is myth-made, media-driven, an inherited memory washed by a generation of tired hands. It's small now, so small, the colours faded and riddled with perfect holes. I shake it out every day and lay it anew over my chewed childhood as a cape or shroud but never a flag.

This Is Not Meant for You

I tore this page from somebody else's book.
It was written in Arabic so I found a man to lend
me his tongue. Left the page splotched with his thickness
& the following words: this was never meant
for you. Your grandfather made that choice & you live
with the ashes of it black on your teeth.
The Uber driver asked me where the local mosque was
real casual like he didn't already know
I had it folded up in a square & carried it everywhere.
It was one of those nondescript places with a
plaque, the kind you need to get close to read
the inscription: *this is not meant for you.*
I tried once to swallow a prayerful palace
but got gum stuck on minarets—these stones
can't be hidden in a body. Everyone knows
where they are. The driver releases me
onto Sydney Road, a replica of home,
all the Leb bread, smoke, & men. I try
not to see my father in them but he is there
no matter where I look, laughing
with the ease of a man never pierced
by a minaret. In each gaping mouth I witness
an old disaster, a rank tooth, a cavity
holding captive my name. I kneel
by the circle of my almost-fathers
not in worship but to listen to what they have
folded in their pockets: a language a sea
a boy never kissed a son never loved a
country that wasn't meant for them
but which they carry everywhere.

On the Way to Sydney

Yellow fields ask too many questions for the sky
to answer. It refuses to lower itself

to what is knowable, a local geography
of facts. Occasionally it will rain

a torrent of dream, a world of water,
more than we need or the fields require.

I can't keep any of it in. My hair gleams.
I am a child again spilling free in Lurnea,

an Arab boy among others, a boyhood of colours,
locust mouths descending on the mall,

heavy with need. Heavier with regret. Or
desire. One thing we never lacked

were questions, bruises. No copper
no security no mother could stump us—I

remember, I wasn't at the scene of the crime
that's not my name, this isn't my house

or my country, I'm telling you I'm not even here
right now, I am somewhere else writing a poem.

It's okay. I have what they call a photogenic memory.
It only retains beauty. Or else what it holds

is made beautiful given enough time.
Like my grandfather feasting on a snake's head

to survive in war-born Lebanon. Like boys
in Coles stuffing pockets with stolen answers.

How to destroy the body slowly

Breathe deep the image
Of the burned body, the spilled

Viscera, the obvious cartilage.
Swallow all the dead children.

Feast your eyes on ruin,
The lunar landscapes of war:

Empty flags, cratered
Cities. Weigh down every last cell

With suffering, but not as Jesus did
In a single span of hours

Wracking flesh & blood, cross & nail,
Into godhood itself. A kind

Of regression. To be human, witness
Each act of woe & sin,

Then live with it

Knowing each blackened moment
Is taking root, is breaking

You. Every day for a hundred years
If you're so lucky

Live with this ordinary
Divinity, live with this death as long as you can,

& waste not a single day on a rose.

Fridays in the Park
(or how to make a boy holy)

& i can't help but notice his hips first, bumbag slung low,
as the train doors open at Roxburgh Park. & i take in the
trackies, his shadowed jaw, the slabs of concrete arcing
over him. & as Arab boys are timeless or else stuck in time,
i breathe easier in their pause, their familiar inescapable
heat. & later, i spot him in the supermarket & know he
knows i'm watching the way a shepherd tends his flock
or the way the ocean shivers when the moon slides onto
its back. & there is no significant body of water in the
suburbs, nothing to drown in yet we drown anyway. & i
take him in the long grass of the park, i taste him in the
weeds, knees wet with mud, the night buzzing with the
deaths of mosquitoes. the wild silence after, mouths heavy
with musk, is complete & even the birds are mute with
love in their nests. there is no song except our huffed
breaths, the shuffle of grass bending beneath us, tickling
skin, the whole world an animal gone quiet. i asked
my aunty about the supernatural hush i felt & she said
the animals stand still in holy awe, they know the Day
of Judgment will fall on a Friday. & this is why neither
of us made a sound, why his fingers bruised my lips to
crush the gasping as one of us disappeared into the other,
why the park bristled with jungle knowing, the kind
with teeth, why it felt like the end of the world &
the beginning, o the beginning of another.

Ameen

I am supposed to begin
with prayer. A snippet
of tongue. Bismillah. If
I am feeling Arab
I extend further
into r-rahmani r-rahim.
Sometimes that means
when I am most scared.
In the name of God the
Most Gracious, the Most
Merciful, I make my tea,
ease my soreness, prep
for sleep. How religious
I sound when in truth
it is one of the few phrases
I know as well as English.
In the grip of a nightmare
it is to Arabic I return
for solace. The scraps
I have left. It is enough
to awaken to sweat.
I fear repetition, that
I might wear the sacred
out of language. Rub
the holy off my mouth.
What then will I face
the devil with in the dark?
Our shared loneliness.
Ask me to love him, I dare

you. I might. I know I must
not go with only this lark,
this irreverent song, spells
empty of heft—this speech
contains only myself, &
nothing of all the other
names God answers to.

How to be a son

My father was for the longest time
a plastic smile locked under the bed.
Before that, he was whatever came
out of my mother's mouth. He was *I'll tell you*
when you're older. He was winding smoke,
a secret name. That fucking Turk.
He was foreign word, distant country.
I gave myself up to her hands which also
fathered; they shaped me into flinch.
Into hesitant crouch, expectant bruise.
Into locked door, CIA black site—
my body unknown and denied to any
but the basest men. I said beat my father
into me please, but he couldn't be found.
And when he was, I wished he remained
lost. He blamed himself for the men I want.
A father can negate any need he thinks
they are the sum of all desires he thinks
absence has a gender. Listen.
You can't backdate love, it destroys
history, which is all that I have & so
like any man, want to abandon.
In the absence of time I will invent
roses, a lineage beyond geography,
then all manner of gorgeous people
who rove in desert and olive grove,
in wet kingdoms, on the hunt for villages
where a boy can love a boy & still be
called son

Sailor's Knot

There are only so many ways a son
can save his mother and I know none.
Hair trailing upward, body twisting
I watched her drown in air. Again.
I still blamed her for not making dinner.
Didn't care for the floundering. Couldn't
tie a sailor's knot nor find a length of
rope. Now between us: borders,
a gulf of time. When I call—
but I don't ever call—she says,
"My son, a lifetime of never submitting,
not to any man or god, yet the angels
I can feel them dancing on my skin.
Who's laughing now?" It's true, we all
knew she had a heart of gold. A pity,
my cousin said, it lies in a drug-fucked
woman. Sometimes I wake at night
choking on the rope I should have made
to save her. Maybe with every beating
she gave me warning
to flee a sinking ship. When she calls—
but she never calls, except for cash—
she says, "My son, the angels are burning
up like tiny candles, and the power's out
so oh I shouldn't enjoy it, but I can see now!"
I'm lying prostrate by the unmade table
in the kitchen, empty plates & knives
floating to the ceiling. Let us both linger
in the image of the record-keepers blazing,

every sin purified. Across the tripwire
lines of country, we sit in the dark
waiting for the call to come or
for a length of rope to unfurl.

Arabs in Space

My aunty arrived in Australia a little Lebanese
girl. She said it was still a time of milkmen
then, of creamy bottles left on doorsteps.
She was not bullied as she learned
English. She dropped out in Year 8
at thirteen years of age
so maybe she got lucky. If so, her belly
was swollen with fortune. An older Arab
boy—not by much but bad enough—
snatched the apples out of her mouth,
trampled all over her garden. Class
is no place for a mother, she learned.
He was a pimp with a stable of hookers
and a constant mother machine at home.
She gave him four kids before his heart
gave out. In life he was their conductor,
orchestrating joyful shrieks. In death
he moves in & out of their gaping
lips. Even cruel men are loved. Children
don't know any better. I still don't. Today
my aunty tells me, "You are not (Arab like)
us." In Islam, in Lebanon, in Turkey,
in all my beginnings the mother is
erased, the earth destroyed by men
by machine   by chance   by design
& there are only the seeds of stars left
running from their own light

What It Is to Be Holy

after & for Kaveh

An Arab of his country and on his country once
said to a boy born in a colony: you too are Arab

I can hear it in your voice. We only knew
each other by what was pushed out.

He said: you have a psychological map,
a pure timeline of 400 years thankful

for family to draw on. I always knew I was ancient.
How else to explain being slowly destroyed,

left to mould in rooms, or being poured over
by people certain they knew what I meant?

He said: the holiest city in the world is quartered
and we can either blame Solomon for the idea

of carving lives in half or else all the plaintiffs
who refuse to love the whole enough.

I have taken to making my god flower
bramble, weed. Maybe to watch divinity

die or to make god observable, small, sweet
something to make honey from, never gospel.

Who was it that said you only write to the land
because the land cannot speak back?

They must not have been fluent in mountains
or an absence of certainty. I have prayed

every day in a language I know only in pieces.
No wonder I have centuries of faith locked

in my hair and nails so long, so matted.
Mattered. I keep doing that. Bleeding

belief, spilling it onto mats and garden beds.
Making love to whatever I consider holy:

the exiled light, the opening in everything,
what came before, spring, poets. Praise

be to God, Lord of all the worlds, even one
in which I am loved and let go.

How to destroy the body slowly (2)

An old white poet, after hearing this, said, "I found myself
Wondering: where is the redemption?"
As if this was a quality inherent to every life, as if it belonged
As if a poem can carry so much
As if the children, before having their foreheads cracked
Open didn't desire an answer
To the question
As if I wasn't desperate to have it waiting here
At the end of my tongue.

Breath

trying to inhale country / sinking & surrounded,
i am lodged like fishbone in a boy's throat, the only
time i become a language, something sayable, tongued.
all around us, muscled farmland tenses flax & convenience
stores sell what we don't have. // what does it say
about us that we call these red interiors "the country"?
where do the rest of us live / if not here. the vast
crumbling cement blocks / lit up with lifeless
lights are still joined at the hip to orchard
& crown, colonialism & cornerstone pub.

               i

splash wild with desire / wherever i am allowed
pierced by the occasional kookaburra's laugh, shrill
on the still, forged morning. // we children of elsewhere
secret ourselves, spilling into a deep ravine / the siren
sound of boys in love. // it resists our touch, the bush
burning as we lie / together, this country & i,
hardness to hardness, stone to bone / drawing a long
gleaming breath like a restless midnight river /
heavy and swollen / with the waterlogged
names of the dead

Birthday

i.

In the evening, my father mistook me
for his father's country. It is the day
of the republic's birth and thus yours,
he said. He was off by a month.
Neither of us could believe so small
a span of hours separated
a boy from a nation.

ii.

Mum manages the month, at least.
She crow-hops annually to another
number, asking, *Is this it?* Always
there are more numbers to be taloned.
Somewhere in the haze of her hashish
a child emerges clutching mountains.

iii.

The year of my birth birthed revolutions.
Eastern Europe convulsed. Walls opened.
A web sprawled under sea, spidered here.
I became me in the land that blew air
into my lungs, a country not of father
or mother. They cannot remember
where they do not belong.

iv.

How many times must one be born
before it is considered final? Poets know
not to mark the day. A thousand births
can take place in a year & a year
on some planets lasts a lifetime.

v.

Some days I wake up as Kafka waking
up as a man up as a son up as a bug
up as a country which, though changed
into some unrecognisable scurrying,
idles in the space it grew up in
unable to leave and with no one
willing to kill it, or look it in the eye
or caress one of its long antennae.
Some days all I hear is the hateful buzz
of its sweet luminous wings.

vi.

I know the day my mother was born
but not the year. And nothing of the man
who thinks of me as his country.
Like any land I have been fought over
with some claiming to love me
more than others, some who are of me
and some who are invaders, new
comers. Those who brutalise my flesh
have also kissed it. Patriots, I suppose.

Everywhere patriots, everywhere
countries burning. I am scared to be
a country in this world.

vii.

Every river, every distant snow-
bound peak, every scraped sky
leans toward its unmaking.
With each gust of wind I grow
outward, dissolving the dirt,
picking borders apart.
Somewhere at the end of this
I will be born, a boy without edges.

Ordinary Things

I was out walking yesterday or perhaps it was today
when a man young as a son spoke under his breath: go
back home, he said, you belong. There, not here. Before
not now. This is not the first time, time was confused.
Tomorrow I go for a jog to let my slab of fat dance
and a woman pushing an empty pram stares,
imagining a past and a place of return I cannot.
I leave the suburbs, and the slithering hills
are nice until they realise I am ignorant
of their names; I am walking away
to the place I live in, and the sun is wetting
my hair, wildebeesting my body, adding weight
to every step. I shop in a convenience store
and the elderly owner nods to me, eyes filmed
over with where he used to be. His mouth
opens, throat bulging, and he ejects a red brick
small and perfectly formed. He says I will need it
some day. To build a bridge or a home? I ask, but
he doesn't seem to think there is a difference.
I put the slick brick in my pocket. It is light as
the wind, heavy as a country. I return
to the house I grew up in and the house tells
there is no succour to be found in the past.
Outside, I see two men in love as a feature
of the landscape, their fingers reaching up
to tender sky. They spit into my hands red
sap I will need some day to mortar. I travel
into my flimsy chest, my lizard brain,
find a refrain of no and go and back and

land and man and home and beneath this
an echo of milk and brick, corn and breakfast,
you know, the ordinary things.

Factoids

My mother sits in a stone house and she burns.
Her father brought his family here to escape history.
When she was young, one of nine, he beat them
with his father's hands. Later, high on heroin,
he became a midnight salesman, selling their jewels
and mattresses. I have no way to verify this.
My grandparents are both home in the mud.
A factoid can be a falsehood or a trivial truth,
it is a hole language allows to have two spirits.

My mother sits in a stone house and she burns.
Sometimes she is the stone, sometimes the flame.
She does not scream. She is a beacon   I record
to use her light as a cudgel, to purple this page.
"I wanted to be an artist once. He wouldn't let me."
Her first husband beat her. He was high on heroin.
He hit her at home. Cracked her skull with a pistol.
Now she forgets her name at least once a day.
He visited her in the hospital as she lay recovering.
He beat her in that bed. I write everything down.

My mother sits in a stone house and she burns.
The house is a villa(ge) in Lebanon. The house is in Villa-
wood. There are photos of my mother before all this—
everyone agrees, she used to be beautiful.
I see her burning, her face and nose and lips curling
up into black paper as she does the dishes
and goes to work and orders takeaway dinner.
There is nothing more beautiful than survival

but I have no one to tell this to, everyone
agrees the present is an ugliness to be ignored.

My mother is not alone in her stone, her fiery
wedding dress. Other daughters go up next to her,
little infernos. They speak cinder and ash,
tongues a brand that sear language into body.
They tell me family has checkpoints vicious
as any country, and not everyone makes it
across or if they do, they lose their names
in a calligraphy ablaze. I wish I had asked
how to choose between a fist at home and
the border, between bruise and bewilderment,
or how to live in a place that is both safe
and wound. Flame and stone. Every word
has two spirits, at least. My mother survived,
and she did not. She can't keep her dreams in,
they pour out the hole in her head a gun left,
a man left, life left—this poem left—open.

My mother sits in the stone house I put her in,
and burns. She could be so much more. I could
tell you of the diamond baked into her tooth.
How she made her smile a gem worth weighing.
I could say she never arrived from Lebanon.
That my grandfather let history burn
his body in Tripoli, and it saved us.
That she drives trucks, knows how to make gelato,
and is always dreaming up new inventions.
That her dogs make her squeal with joy.
Inside my stone house, these things seem trivial
or false, but I tell you they are true.

Chances

"I want to go my country." My country wants to go
Me. Don't go anywhere, my grandmother warns.
Her country is waiting. When she left it for this one,
Few Turks had gone so far. She slept on folded up
Blankets. "I no know English." I know how
I misunderstand her   sometimes
Purposefully. Then, everyone
Spoke with their bodies. She mastered
The low talk of the eyebrow, the lullaby of batted
Lash, the harsh frisson of hands open,
Clenched. Nobody bothered to learn her
Body. The nation
Skipped that lesson. Nothing to see her(e). "No
TV, no newspaper, no phone. I no have nothing,"
She says with envy. What a thing to gild
A tongue! She worked by day
In a factory, worked at home by night
First with her children, then their own.
"Yes," she exclaims, "me when I working I love.
No nice sometimes, but nice." She shrugs, & even
Her shrugs are historic. I sense a levelling in them.
Everything in her world is 50-50. She is never
Happy, or angry or sad or living or dying. Always
She tells me, 50-50. I fit so easy in this splittage
I am giddy. There were many other
Migrants labouring
Beside her, all of them with a country
Waiting. Greek, Italian, Indo, Filipino, Spanish.
She prayed in the factory; the Muslims took shifts

To cover God. She never went uncovered. She lost
Two daughters, two sons, her husband of 53 years.
"Nine years ago
He go." Their bed has emptied since.
She takes the couch, a long bench that fits only her.
Every visit I visit my ancestors. In her eyes Turkey
Sings in a way Erdogan could never imagine. She
Brings out photos of the dead. "Look, you look
Just like him. And him." A hymn.
Every visit I visit myself
Only to shed him at the door. I invoke the past
When it suits. I fold it up to soften a hard bed.
Her apartment has a flat screen live-streaming
Turkish TV. Her mobile bides its time. The photos
Gather, multiply. "Now I have everything," she says,
"God gives." And the loss in her could make paintings
Weep. "But inside?" She shrugs. Her country is
Waiting, she says, and there is a 50-50 chance
She is right.

Instead, Memory

i.

I know a flower   is not a weapon   but the possibility
for harm remains. I've cut myself open on fields

looking for the borders I heard were waiting there.
I've cut open the fields looking for this
bludgeon   I used to believe I could destroy

or wield to my own end. Now I only want to see the snakes
biting at my feet, to care for where I step. I worry
any act of extinction will warp the ecosystem. Surely

I am obliged to love what I cannot erase. My memories
ache for this to be true. They do not want to die.
Even my darkest knowing seeks the light

as a new kind of mother. I ask the light how
to behave. It should know, it has been around at least
the block touching gentle what can be touched

including, remarkably, me
the house, some trees. It kills nothing,
shepherding even the night to sleep
for a while. I envy what returns.

What might it feel like to save what I see? To bring
it back, through memory, unscathed. Instead,
whatever I alight upon becomes a violence: my boy

-hood featured three queens & a carousel of kingless
men. None of them knew how to touch without
wounding and all of them touched

instinctively. This is what they taught me,
to trust the lesson the gasp imparts. Yaani I strip
back the skin not to bare the fault lines

but to know: it is possible to ask too much
of a colour, which is to say light. Together

they insist on revealing blood, as if blood,
especially the human kind, can't tell a lie

or turn against itself, when its first narrative
was one of expulsion, and its first product was Cain.

Do you see? My grandfather and his children, my mother
& my body, my body and itself. Always turning

away from a country. The truth is: it is easy to give
trauma a body. To a body. I mean, it wants to be made

visible, a transformation often
mistaken for a miracle, a healing action. Like light

I love to dance before mirrors naked, rude,
dripping. This is what you are here for: the epiphany

of my flesh, the violent manifesto, the prophecy divined
through diaspora, the spilled guts of sacrificial

animals opening a new future,
the many born of one.

ii.

I strip back my flesh my bloody ego. Come
meet me at the juncture of knee & history,

here my bestial memories cluster
in glorious hymnal each beak and snout

and jowl closeting a secret, an ordinariness,
a child, a lust. I rule over them, an abject king,

an ungovernable queen with a heel on every
throat. Don't listen to me. Hear the humming

insects digging in, which is the sound of Mum
gargling in the kitchen   snorting a line
straight out of this suburban kingdom

and into a place of her own. I keep inventing
a place for her to own. My ego again.
It never lasts, my fantasy, be it Lebanon

or a bone forest or an unlikely
evergreen, a thriving joyful something—

instead, memory
overwhelms everything & I see a coastal city

that spells her father's addictive name, that shreds
her girlhood   where she staggers through the heat,

an axe in hand, ready to make beautiful
his body with an old ruin & slake

a different kind of thirst. I have learned
to ask too much of beauty, to beg it

for vengeance
and still, it answers.

iii.

I strip back my bones, leave only a sovereign
melancholia, a light in pieces, a glittering I don't dare

hold. In shattered mirrors my father is still
alive, his eyes a web of red, a laugh curving

his lips, waiting for me to turn and acknowledge
his terrible throne. This is the trouble

with faith, it fathers and leaves you
with children who refuse to die

Out on the Way to Melbourne

i.

a boy embalmed by the sun
    cricket bat held high

pools of mud by spent tractors
      and unspent men

stray cattle gracing the grazing
    fields, oozing methane

a winding wooden spine nailed to hills,
      a continuous crucifixion—

i pass over it untouched, a desire
    thrumming through

half-heard half-hearted
      lacking the conviction

of this ugly flower, a clenched fist
    of beaten gold.

ii.

this morning, i woke up & forgot
    how to pray.

i scrambled for god
        the correct sequence of words
the rhythm

        beneath it all. i strained

& mumbled, a note here, an amen there
        like the night before, sweating
hallelujah in heat

bodies like confessional boxes long
        unused & full of secrets.

as the day withdraws   i am out
        in the canola fields, trying to recall
what faith is and to resist

the voice softly saying, throw yourself
        into the nearest burning bush.
do not listen if it speaks to you—
                                    simply burn.

iii.

i leave country behind
sick pastoral ghosts   & mad cows
uttering *fag fag fag*

        or maybe it was fog,
soft song of confusion. i
    don't blame the animals,

they only repeat what they hear.
    back in my devastated home
land, i am a vulgar prince

with an invader's tongue
    in my mouth & i love it.
i go to the olive groves

ready to wear a dress of flame

    and a hundred pitted eyes say:
        history is one long receipt &
all our names are on it.

A Beautiful Child

after Jericho Brown

You are not as tired of diaspora
poetry as I am of the diaspora. Sometimes

I thank God that I was born inside an American
-made tank. Sometimes I weep within

the beast. My uncle works on the railroads
and goes home to his nuclear family loathing

my queerness from afar. He and I tend
our silence, a beautiful child

until it speaks. Another uncle is a guard
with two ex-wives and a secret love

of comic books. Tragedy made him the head
of his family too soon. *Don't weep for your dad*

he said, *weep for me.* "You didn't know him
like I did." I have a third uncle, a mechanic

who visits his home in Lebanon every year
& now I must admit English has failed me.

I should say kholo, my mother's brother.
I should say umja, my father's brother

so you know which branch of the tree to cut—or
cherish. My uncles are doused in industry, good sons

of the State. They get on with what needs
getting on. Language is their least favourite

daughter. They use their mouths for breath
and do their best to forget the world

outside. I think they love where they come
from but in truth, I have never heard them

say so, except to mutter they do not want
to pay taxes in two countries come on

one is killing them already &
isn't that enough

Choose Your Own Erasure

In a Field She Twirls, Arms Akimbo & the World Stops
to Watch (or: Happiness)

In this poem, my mother has no purpose
beyond existing, beyond beauty, beyond
dancing beneath the stars. Let me give
way before meaning, let me incoherent,
let me give her this one shining moment.

In a Field We Twirl, Arms Akimbo & the World Stops
(or: Grief)

In this poem, trauma is not the villain
to whom all blame is allocated, trauma
has no cape, no moustache to twirl, no
body to act through, no blood to poison
& my mother knows precisely the harm
she is causing. She knows its name.
She calls it: his story. She makes it ours.

In a Field, the World (or: Rage)

In this poem, a country is unwinnable,
unwoundable, unowned. It never
justifies killing people. It does not want
our bodies. It lives, and loves the living.
It knows no other way and resists
whenever we try to teach it otherwise.

In a Field (or: Denial)

In this poem, absence is recalibrated.
Absence is a deer springing over logs.
It is flighty but incapable of damaging
you intangibly. It can still stand still
on a road, and cause a car to crash
or swerve into a monstrous silence,
the kind that follows any arrival.

In (or: Acceptance)

In this poem, I am a boy desiring
other boys without consequence,
I suck dick with abandon, fear free
from my tongue. I am beholden
not to desire but to myself, my love,
the women, the men, all of us
fixated on the thresholds
of bliss or a way to displace
for a second or an hour
the exit that haunts the body.

Federation (Square)

This place reminds me of a Holocaust
memorial, an uneven jumble of stones,
architecture twisting my vision.
Only this is meant to be beautiful.
I don't know what it remembers,
if it can speak to that other square
in a distant city burdened with memory,
to the makers of it & to those who desire
to dip a slender milky foot into history,
a kind of accessible suffering captured
on camera. You know the solemn ones
in their duty-free sunglasses or else
unbearably in love, smiling.
There is no good way to be here
or anywhere else. At least there
are trams, trains, buses, and cabs;
we need as many ways to flee
as possible. You can leave this poem
every 8 minutes in any number of directions
new meaning arrives. Perhaps it's better
to say arises, that it struggles out the earth or
wafts free off the wide back of the mud
brown river or falls from the long low head
of a tree. New doesn't mean better,
remember once the other is elsewhere,
it's hard to get back. Maybe impossible.
I don't blame the open for what comes.
Everything reminds me of the dead.

My ghosts are as noisy as the colony
of gulls pecking food from my hands.

The Lost Arabs
for my dear Najwan

In the kingdom of lost Arabs, every rock is a beautiful
separatist until you spit on it.

In some cultures spit is a benediction.
Give me the waters of your tongue, any wet word

can soothe a silent throat and mine
keeps closing over my mother, grandmother,

and even my slowest, least kind cousins
who can speak with the thick voice of our people

and who, with each sloshing mouthful, locate
themselves in our country. My teeth

dream of the three nations that yellow
their bone. I wet their edges,

a clueless cartographer who has never known a hill
or a river that wasn't stolen from someone

and so can never know their true shape.
When I look at our names, all I see are squiggly lines.

Would you believe I keep trying to find the poetry
in a wound? How foolish. How graceless. And yet:

a man who knows his history told me it was in my blood.
What idiot put it there?

Maybe this is why I have spilled so much of it on the blade
of authenticity. Cut down

those I deemed false, all the others I loved—and love—
but refused to become. Every day

my certainty collapses. That I am lost. Or can be found.
That there is such a thing as Arab.

None of this is real, it exists only in your mind,
the stone I cleaved with this sword.

Pull it out if you can, if you dare a kingdom
awaits the steady

hands of a new butcher. I confess myself
unequal to the task.

Where God Is

The jihadi in his cargos and camo, his fake beard and sunnies, stands bowlegged in the desert/ed parking lot. He has no quiver of arrows, but a belt of gold teeth, a wicked / smile looped around his chest. He looks like my cousin / as he squints at me, ready to spit. / "Where can you find God?" / he says. They ask this of every poet or faggot or Westerner / my not-cousin assures me / they are all poets. He swears he is not my cousin / refuses me his name. / I am sweating like a used horse. I hate games / I can't win. / There are two answers. The first is now/here, as glory is beyond small / animals. We live in the absence of divinity, and by our actions / hope to create an echo here, to call it back. The other / answer is everywhere: heaven / in torn Coke cans, in my dirty / armpit, in laundry, in a brothel / deluged with rain, in every single breath sucked in by living things, the dead / echoing. I say nothing / full of the stink of myself. The man / who could be my cousin—this is to say I could love him—laughs, puts a cold black mouth to my ear / and I hear, "Listen. / You will find God here."
Then the angels started barking

Searchlight

I lay above this poem as I lay above my body
watching it all go wrong. I, the Arab cannot

enter this space. I, the Arab am not just
an Arab. I have another mad blood

product of a con man and a junkie—sorry,
substance abuse(r)—I, the Arab am

familiar with a relentless need, with never
having enough, a cracked cup

that mocks notions of being half of anything.
Whatever I have dribbles out, dews

the fracture. I, the Arab am surrounded
by a blast radius where a tree should be

& so I am always in mourning. I desire
the shade of those long branches,

the particular shape of a hundred names
whether all of them were shady sand-fuckers

turning tricks in a trashy gutter or worse,
capitalists, which is to say, soldiers

of fortune. Anyway, someone surely must
have been good, or known the joyous

thrum of a song or being held as a son
by a human who loves you

even if later on they kicked in your teeth.
None of this is what I wanted

to say in search of my inheritance,
that sad will-o'-wisp, leader of the lost

and soon to be drowned. I want to drink
in these marshes, make my mouth glow

with mushroom bloom but my jaw,
so like my grandfather's, is cracked

& leaking. This is my legacy, dear
children: an endless migration

to what was or might have been,
the manacles of a horrid imagination

and somewhere I swear to God
the Most Merciful, a smile, praise.

Every Day

Every day I say a prayer for Palestine
And every day a dog runs away with it
Vanishing down an alley, tail wagging
To benefit who knows which wretch.
I tell myself it doesn't matter who receives
The gift of my kindness. Such lovely lies
We bestow upon ourselves. Sometimes
I am the dog fleeing with a bastard's
Love clenched in my slavering jaw.
Sometimes I am the one curled at the end
Of an alley, blessed by the unexpected
Warmth of a snuffling mouth telling
Me I am not forgotten. Every day
I say a prayer for Palestine

Do Not Rush

to make a judgment.
You can savage a body at speed.
A city can be ruined in an hour.
A love of decades dashed in a second.
It takes nine months to start a life.
It should take as long to end one.
After a trigger is pulled and before
a bullet lands, give nine months
to the target to welcome the hole,
to accept the blood, the blunt lead,
the new body. I know it is possible
to allow a death to gestate. Watch
time mushroom out from a bomber
and seasons unfurl on the city below.
Spring in Baghdad to winter in Aleppo,
one final semester of learning, a retreat
by a river, time enough to be thankful
for old books and DVDs borrowed,
to study the bullet or the blast with
a lover's eye. It seems a short goodbye
but last year alone America dropped
26,171* bombs on brown bodies,
on our trees and animals and homes.
That's 235,539 months or 19,628 years
to process the devastation of one.
Honestly, I am unsure of the maths.
Give or take a week, millenniums
are still owed to the lost. I don't know
how to calculate for the land or

the numbers for the unlucky survivors,
the dust-strewn rubble-reapers looking
for family in red rocks, for burned
paper that might hold a shred of name,
for safe waters that will not drown
them, for borders that will not cut
their feet or demand they unstitch
history from their backs. Call it
an ugly flag. Plant a new one
in their mouths. This kind of loss
has not been measured, it has no body
count, but we have all the time
in the world to weigh it now.
We have all the time in the world.

---

*When I wrote this poem in 2017, I was referring to statistics from 2016. As I
write this in 2018, I can tell you that in 2017 America dropped 40,000 bombs.
From 2014 to 2017, at least 94,000 bombs. In my lifetime alone, the sheer ton-
nage of destruction and chaos that has been unleashed on majority Muslim or
Arab nations has been nothing short of catastrophic, year after year of stagger-
ing violence that the population of Western countries seem to accept. Go back
further, past my lifetime, my mother's, and into my grandfather's and you will
still find ample military campaigns and Western-backed violences to highlight
the sustained injustice against Arab peoples. You could not do this to those you
saw as fully human. Though I had not the heart to seek out the full body count
of Iraqis, Afghanis, Syrians, Yemenis, Palestinians—the refugees drowned in
wave after generational wave of forced migration, of certain death at home or a
bleakening hope abroad—the munitions alone tell a deadly, horrifying story.

AT THE SITE OF THE
FUTURE MEMORIAL

I will learn every dead body is impossibly foreign.
Still, their names my name will be lodged
in throats. I will replace the lost with my blood.
I have never given so much of myself before
and, having fucked men this year, usually
I would not be allowed. *Aren't you all the same*
will echo through loudspeakers as the guilt
-stricken meander in, awe-splotched &
delirious. Look at what we did. Look
how easy it was.

There will be a fountain splashing blackness &
haphazard TVs showing only National
Geographic. I remember laughing at my father who was
fond of invoking the Afghani kings in our blood.
He burned to be special, to etch glory in these bones.
What does it say about me that I call on the erased,
the shrapnel song of gone? Now that my father is gone
I will try to make a crown for him to wear
and say without irony that we kingdomed Western
Sydney, we wore exquisite costumes. Though imaginary,
it will be rich with gems. I keep annihilating homelands
by turning my back   I keep surviving somehow.

I may not be alive for the sight of the future
memorial, in which case it is important to note
I am a writer and to write is to squander life.
It is the only reason I have a place here.

Aren't you all the same? I don't recognise
the photos here, and I do. Some of the legs
blown off bodies, those with jeans still on,
could be mine. I use memory to make them
walk again. God, do not let me anywhere
near memory, I beg of you. I keep using it
as a weapon. It is the only thing I know
how to do and that should tell you everything.

AT THE SITE OF THE
FUTURE MEMORIAL

I will illegally build my own Statue of Liberty
alone night and day for a hundred years if need be
and need be
so when I am done I can blow her head off
and fill the jagged cup of her skull
with tears that will not freeze
nor dissipate but always drip
down her stern jaw, her arms, her perfect
dress and into the upturned thirst
of anyone unlucky enough to stand in her shadow.
She has a poignant purpose, yes—for example
if you tip her over she will be an Ark
for all the animals liberty has room for,
but I would be lying if I said I'm doing it
for any reason other than getting to fuck her
face up without reprisal.

AT THE SITE OF THE FUTURE MEMORIAL

Consider all the other memorials & know the difference
between a memorial and a moratorium, so much lies
in a name. Consider the many still in construction,
those never thought of, the denied, design
in your mind all the palaces of sorrow
you can stand—one for all who came before,
for those who remain, for the Great Barrier
Reef, for roses, for madness, and all extinctions.
Though we have none of the stones necessary
each house in my family fits the bill.
We just don't charge admission

AT THE SITE OF THE
FUTURE MEMORIAL

I will play footage of American Gods on my phone—no,
not those hideous drones delivering eternities
everywhere—I mean, the episode
with the hung djinn in New York & the salesman,
two hairy men made cosmic with desire, eyes of fire
so we can all see a man give to another man his flame
instead of blood & come away unscathed. Unless
you count love, unless you count its edge, its sweat.
Some will say this is an indulgence, an excess,
but of course the fact he has a big dick is essential,
not just because it's beautiful but because it is a weapon
and because if a man possessed is to be lessened by gay
sex there must be compensation, a balancing, a coming
to the senses. I can't turn my criticism off. Too often
I mistake cynicism for criticism. My eyes are burning
again   I watch them fuck into astral glory   again
I watch them remake my world   again I weep
as I never have for death.

AT THE SITE OF THE FUTURE MEMORIAL

I will tear up the usual, the piles of bodies, the oasis,
the keffiyeh, the dishdasha, the ahwa, the ululation,
the princedom, the mosque, the minaret, the minutes,
the taxi driver, the donkey, the lecher, the angry Arab
Israeli conflict, the hookah, harem, the bloody stones,
the swanky hotel, pool-side glitz, the rugs, the Rolex,
the AK-47, the camo, ammo, the fucking politicians,
the successful literate migrant, the sons of despair,
the oil fields, the hijabs, the thugs, the clubs,
the Quran—everything, I will ruin as I was ruined
once. This, too, is usual. Wait. Turn up the music.
Play it again, life, the ugly, the pulse. Let me dance
in the static, cover the bullet holes in feathers
from every bird. Let me embrace the terrifying
mirage, the sick self. Let the whole building
shrug me off   and fly

Waiting for the American Spring

Everyone has the blizzard on their lips.
Batten down. Turn the word over:
a large or overwhelming number of things
arriving suddenly. What could be
more appropriate to sum up the American
condition? A state of being still arriving
suddenly, welcome or not. Cold corpses
line the streets, some alleys, maybe
a park or two—a few no doubt hang
in a frozen lake, swordless, wondering
how it was they ate their dreams &
still went hungry. I'm talking bodies
concaved with wanting, talking ice
-mantled animals. Small losses mount,
small squalls merge. It's never sudden,
not really—more an accumulation.
You can talk about it before every dawn
and still be shocked by the force
when it hits. Another meaning: *denote*
a violent blow. As when wind uproots
an oak, or a boy shakes another boy
until his teeth shatter. There are cities
here without clean water. Black bodies
shaken until they shatter in the street
as they have since the first blizzard—
meaning: *whiteout*—stole them. Now
the world winters a storm where the stolen
refuse to remain lost, buried in snow.
They get up on lips, the as yet unghosted

armed with the tinder of names. Think
of all the bodies shivering across country,
the azan bottled up in blue throats,
the borders of *suddenly* always cutting. When
will this arrival stop overwhelming? You
can't build a wall around a season,
a forest of bone, a land always dying.
Look to your bleached plains and ask
how much longer can you last
without real food or a sprig of green?

A Moratorium on Cartography

Burn all the maps. Forget about want
I need unspoiled long-&-latitudes.
Some unguttered earth, a place
even the stars haven't touched
where I can come up for air,
where there is no such thing
as drowning, and no killing
but in which I can still die
a natural death. Impossible
dreams are for young men.
I am not as young as necessary.
It could be a dream this large
requires age, and I am not old
either. Countries are unwieldy
things not to be made alone.
I wish someone told me that
before I started building beaches.
It's got nothing to do with land,
that gorgeous animal. I just forgot
the people. Maybe I meant to &
I should make the most of these
acacias, the long tapering bushes
before they inevitably burst
into flame, the language not
of gods but of man. Prometheus
knew. It is a lesson we unlearn
as often as we can: alphabets
are all sinuous destruction.
All we wanted was to sear

a moment, a handprint, a hunt
into the rock to let it know
our names, unaware naming
the world would also end it.
My country resists language.
It does not want to know you.
It has its own knowledge, and no
holes for flags. It can't be
stolen. I have carved it out
of freedom. Now what it means
to be free is in pieces and there
is no such thing as peace.

Tinder

I would swipe right on torture.
This is not a great start

to the relationship. The truth is best
saved until it's too late or too hard

to reject: prevent the body
from flinching in status-preserving instinct,

get it to swallow the poison
of a toxic beginning, a vaccine for history

that necromantic motherfucker always
trying to resurrect itself, to live

again now. We are always saying honesty
is necessary but nobody talks about when

or where this razor should be applied,
as in the case of a poem. Poems do not need

an I to work the way the system needs
an eye to work, one for you & nobody

else. You work better when you only look
out for yourself. Stay focused

as you move the blade: I would swipe right
on torture. I know it happens

with each scoop of cereal, each crunch
of sugar electrocuting happiness

up my spinal column—somewhere
someone is being electrocuted

for real and I carry living
on because this is the price of doing

business, which in my case is writing
poems and having one eye and

trying to stay focused on the wobbling spoon
of conductive metal aimed at my teeth.

I put torture in a box and I hide the box
(which is heavier than my body)

under my bed, and I wonder how
I'm going to get someone to fuck me

on a mattress full of screams.

Among Bloody Oracles

Time constantly remembers
the man tall as anything, his hair electrified
worms, his hands all knuckles & bone,
clutching a red white blue striped bag.
He stood outside my boyhood & I, small
as anything, approached his unstatic
body. Turning, one eye wild, one tame,
he opened his mouth and time zombie
climbed its way out his gaping lips.
"My parents were cut down by the SS,"
he said, then popped out a marbled eye,
I forget which one, and planted it deep
across my palmed life & love & loss
lines. I closed my hand over its hard
vision, looked up into his black hole
where a smaller, sadder me wrote
this poem. I did not know how to say
sorry for what I could not comprehend.
I gave back his world, touched now
by young flesh, to plug the wound.
Wet with sweat, it would blossom
next spring, the sweetest flower ever
to leaf. I tremble on the edge of carpal
swelling out in concentric whorls
of luck, that bitter fruit. Today stalks
rotting memory, pecking out chunks
of spoil. The past does the same,
their blood mixing together as I
walk down the supermarket aisle,

pick an apple off the mushed face
of some unfortunate, grab a bottle of
condensed fiscal uncertainty, and pay
at the counter, a man in uniform
who looks like a young woman smiling
but is a man in uniform cutting down
a body in a camp somewhere. They
do not notice I have given an eye to pay,
but place it in the cash register full
of all the other eyeballs rolling together
in the soft wilful dark.

Self-Portrait as Poetry Defending Itself

The birds tell me the nest is crucial but can't hold
all of us. Stay on the wind as long as it will carry
you, then find a home, build it from everything
a tree has let go. My aunty tells me forgetting
has a survival value by saying nothing at all.
This is only what I tell myself with her mouth:
in Arabic, the word for mercy and forgiveness
is the same. Some birds use lit sticks to fan the
flames of a bushfire, and feast on what escapes.
Those who live tell me there is no such thing
as escape, that once you've been burned
everything resembles a flame. Who in this
story deserves mercy and at what cost?
Should the bird go hungry, the tree unburned
the air untasked with speeding on death, or me
the fool at the end of it all trying to make sense
of suffering. This is only a replica. The pain came
and went, yet here I am invoking it again, a nest
I re-create to burn over and over until I learn
I cannot be saved or forgiven for what I lived
through. I keep looking to the world for a salvation
it has never known, keep winging toward a word
like water, a mirror, a mover, a matter, a mother,
a word closer to but not as smothering as solace.
I never want to arrive at a sweetened language,
or to speak the unfindable word, my sole desire
is to hold it between my teeth, and to be held.

Extermination

The man, of unknown origin, revealed himself
as Arab when he took his shoes off at the door.
There were other signs but I cannot tell you.

He arrived armed for chemical warfare
as we all do. His socks were soft, grey.
We told him not to worry, the floor

was tiled, easy to clean. He insisted on leaving
his muddiness behind. Flexed his toes on white.
I followed the tense up his hairy brown

legs, until his shorts hid the muscled rest.
He sprayed as he went, tank of poison in hand.
There were rat droppings in the ceiling.

A crunchy rain fell, startled cockroaches
waking to light and death as every child does.
They kissed his feet and for that I envied them.

Landscaping

The grass loops long outside my window. Sags into itself. A thousand lithe men bowing in one direction, a lone sunflower here & there draped over their knees. Little sluts. I forget to cut them down. It is winter now and the sea of green is bright with death as if begging for the attention of the blade. I can't afford a lawnmower. Still, I picture myself pushing a fat hungry thing on the yard, shirtless, a thick beast among snaking weeds. I'm unsure what to kill out here. What qualifies as weed: nasty useless unflower, purposeless growth—and anything that isn't beautiful has no purpose, I've heard.

The grass though, if grass it is, has such luscious curls. It tells there is beauty in neglect. My baby cousins have curly hair, all little Lebs. Some grow out of it. Some are cut down before they can. The air mows the earth. Sky rake. Cloud gardener. The land lord is unhappy. This is not Greece, he said. What a shit sea. There is no one here to save from it. I want the waters to rise higher still, submerge my body. I want to stalk naked through its soft hands, lone sunflower looking to spread against lengths. To queer this domestic Eden. A mirage. There are no persuasive snakes in my yard, just one crab apple tree bristling with overripe cheeks splotched red, rotten cores. They bob on the sea, fallen fruit, baby heads. The cold is creeping in. There is no one to save here I whisper as I go over every inch with my mouth and lovingly tender the green.

How to sleep

My cousin the farmer is laden with death
he tells me each morning he checks the chickens
while I sleep. The weaklings need killing,
so he walks among them, dawn-spectre,
and takes their lives. It has to be done,
he tells me. While I sleep, the long sheds
hot as summer's guts are home to lone
acts of kindness. Among ten thousand
fluffed bodies, his eyes hawk upon
the others, the strange-winged, hobbling,
he tells me: I get a little rope, noose
it round their necks and hang them
from the ceiling. He laughs at my belief.
I'm kidding. I just snap their necks
like this—his huge hands twist the air
so sharp I'm surprised it doesn't crack.
Ravens haunt the nearby treetops
and foxes stalk the feathered earth
outside the sheds the survivors yet
live, for now. My cousin tells me
Cain and Abel were the first
to farm, to keep and raise animals
as sacrifice. A lamb for God. A brother
for the devil, who taught a man how
a stone could crack a skull, but not
why. When the devil brought news
of her son's downfall, Eve said, "Woe
to you. What is murder?" "He eats not.
He drinks not. He moves not," said he

in reply. Many days I have lain
as if felled by a fallen angel
unable to move   I tell my cousin
maybe I lose half my days
in penance, maybe I die a little
every night, for this. The absence
of a brother. He walks away
from belief. He will sleep tonight
in the hot house, lying in the reek
of their living. He will be covered
in a cloak of wings, hear the song
of too-many hearts, and his hands
will be stoneless, still, all of them
waiting for the crack of dawn.

Citizen of—

One desultory howl is what I imagine singing
out the throat of the grey wolf separated
from his mate by a wall neither had dreamed of.
There are so few of them left it falls to me
to dream of a muzzle unbothered by country,
summoning the music of the lost. Wolves
understand territory, borders of lifted leg
but not of stone. Maybe the Americans will
walk along the dirt and drench the invisible.
Nobody consulted the wolf, spotted owl, jaguar,
thick-billed parrot, barred tiger salamander,
Mount Graham red squirrel, ocelot, or armadillo
as to which passport they would deign to keep.
Of course they are citizens of everywhere,
at least in part. Some species must move to live,
and that means they must also have enemies.
An angry landlord. A jilted lover. A neighbour
who couldn't bear to be outshone or out-howled.
So maybe Arizona's no good anymore or Mexico is
the go. For some love is a destination to be winged
toward or from—it's never where you originate.
Others just want to eat or stretch warmth
out another season. Scientists haven't measured
or mapped the devastation a wall would trap
in place, but the lights at night would lure millions
of monarch butterflies to flutter topaz gold
no more and fall to drape the earth like autumn

leaves. Bilingual beauties*, I don't need to imagine
their howl—everyone will hear it echoing
in time. Listen. It is tickling your ear even now.

---

*I trust you to know this isn't about butterflies. OK, I don't trust
you.

How to destroy the body slowly (3)

I have wasted so many days on roses
On all sorts of ragged blossoming &
I will waste so many more—

The Exhibition of Autobiography

I put history in a cabinet where it can do the least
damage. I make sure to buff from time to
time. It cannot be less than

glamorous. We keep paying for it, anyway. Maybe
this is why it lives. I am obsessed with
the past the same way a victim

is obsessed with their killer, not their body
but the origin story, the motive where
the end began. In a dream

I explain this to my mother as I throttle
her neck, and she smiles. Finally,
we are a family. I won't say

when I let go, only that I don't know how
to look to a future I am certain
doesn't include me.

Everything is changing now that I am in love.
I'm still here, still sworn to sorrow's geas
but the exit has inched closer.

Kennel Light

She was a rescue. A master trembler
she fears the door as much as
the wall. I let her out of the cage.

She bolts toward the light, the new. I wish
I could charge from this world into another
instead of crawling. I've done it at least once

before surely. Men make her anxious.
I watch from the couch. Movement excites fear.
She bounds toward my feet, backs down

bounds again. Fighting herself. Nameless
in the way of stray animals. Language
urges a response: call me a dog

or donkey or boy with the right tone
and I'll come running. My mother proved that.
She made me a mongrel often

enough. The dog presses her neck on
my foot. She twists against my shoe, moving
around as if any touch is better than

no touch. Who called you a rescue?
I croon, as the cur rams her throat
on my sole, tail wagging, desperate.

I curl up into a ball so she can't use me
as an instrument of cruel memory.
I hear the lock click shut. I whine, turn.

The world has always been this small.

The dog and I disagree on the ethics
of touch. I only want to be seen,
and on my greedier days, heard.

Our desires collide into nothing,
proof we're both dumb bitches
in the end, jumping at the past,

running in our dreams, barking at
all our animal instances, the hidden
collar nestled against skin.

No Goldblum, No Matter

I want you to know I have seen a thousand dinosaurs
on a barn floor, most of them an outrageous yellow,
while some were black and all of course newborn,
shifting from thick talon to thick talon chittering
in anticipation of a stranger world than they knew.
You will say, they are not dinosaurs anymore.
You will say, look at their bodies. The body knows.
And it's true, they were small and fluffy
and Jeff Goldblum was nowhere to be seen
and the place swam in waves of oily heat
and I could walk the dimensions of their universe
and the walls would be so easy to knock down—
walls always are—but bodies do not *know*
anything. They remember, they imagine.
The day I saw a thousand dinosaurs, I knelt
in the soft mulch and whispered their history
and saw a raptor light come into their being,
which is to say, emerge from forgetting
as I once did. I know from whence I came.
I tore the stuffing out of a bus seat with my teeth
when the memories first transformed me,
and after that I saw the borders of my world
and laughed at their crude lines thinking
they knew the limits of my flesh.
Only carnage can come from such certainty.
I am never what I expect myself to be,
one day a man, the next a strange reverie.
If this is true of the cosmos, we must worry
what ours recalls, what it might still invent,

what was lost. It could be legendary,
a vicious animal or something small
enough to survive whatever is coming.

How to endure the final hours

It is so strange to witness an animal / dying. More than living, that is, breath remains / our working assumption even in new/found species. We look for life, always. Here & beyond the stars. Cut a ram's throat if you disagree. It is harder than the line suggests / its sinew is tough to cut. See the blood spurt from the part / a viscous flood. Feel the wool / scratch against your bunched palm. The frantic whites of its eyes / look to find / God or meaning, it kicks at clumps of mud, mussing / worms, crushing ants, making a mess / of the earth, snorting mist / into the early light / its nostrils wide & wet, bleating at the air / as it folds, gently at first, then in a rush. // Every death is violent to the life around it, seeks to take as much as it can. / As it ends you / will strain to see mortality disproven, a twitch in its flank, a spar of grass bending to breeze or last / huff as hot red deepens into black around your boots. Do not worry / if you find nothing. This is what I tell myself. Do not / worry. The search / alone is beautiful.

How to destroy the body slowly (4)

When I am bleeding out sure
As a body cratered by a blast
I often think of God as explosive
& that having faith tears holes
In your chest to make room
For itself. It will kill
Whatever it finds there, even
Kindness. Faith is an old bear
In the chamber of your heart. It is
Best left sleeping, a warm pile of
Itself, a furry back to rest on
In winter. Awake, it is hungry
& needs something to die
That it might live.

Self-Portrait of What Graces the Night

The moon does not identify
as moon. Nobody has tried
to crush it. Who would define
their body as less than another?
As orbiting shine, as hole?
Earth hollered at it and yeah,
it knows when it gets called,
naming is a bitch like that—
so it pulls back, makes refusal
a circle, a virtue, a kindness.
Not-Moon said, I own your sky
sometimes with only a fingernail.
Not-Moon said, your waters are
mine. Who you calling moon?
I am the one looking down,
the first to see you and say
dirt. Trust a child to disrespect
its parent. I lie beneath the night
an astronaut in an alternate life,
thinking what I would have said
had I been the first man
to step on it. Maybe: a' salaam
wu alaikum. *Peace be upon
you*, bright light, sweet spirit.
Or maybe just: ahlan, shu ismek?

Blues

Listen: countless days I've looked at heaven
and imagined the cupped hand of it closed.
I have made braille of the stars and divined
a message there for the reviled, a whispered
no, not for you. I have seen the moon
as scalpel, as wet white blade, as glaring,
as waiting hole to be plunged into, as drop
pearling on the tip, as well of wonder, as coin
to pay for my eventual passage into after.
I have made it my enemy, over and over.
I don't know how often I helled blue heaven,
made of it a furnace. Such hate I've sketched
all on my own into the willing curve of world
and still, every night, the loving dark sweeps
in, and still, every morning delights again or
weeps in woollen bunches, giving life
to life. This should not surprise you.
Everywhere, the earth wallows beneath
the weight of all that men imagine of it,
all that we graffiti the bright mirror with,
and everywhere the wind laughs
at how easy it is to wipe our cruelties
away. Now I just want you to know
my loves I opened my mouth
and swallowed the sky not
because a man scrawled rejection on it
as men have done since forever began
but because it was beautiful and I wanted
to taste every flavour of blue, every cloud.

Nature Poem

I keep pitting people against flowers. It's an unfair contest.
     I keep pitting myself
against myself. You see where I'm going with this.
     The notion of the land is never
as compelling as the land. What you say about my body is
     nothing next to my fat nipple,
its hairy crown. The degree of love people have for dogs,
     cats, birds, roses, and other
demonstrably inhuman bodies is astounding. It is so easy to
     love what isn't you,
what is removed, what is alien, what speaks another
     language, aloof or affectionate,
what brandishes another colour. This goes against what we
     learned. That love is
difficult. That we must steal to know each other better,
     to empathise. That we are knowable.
That cohabitating requires cages. I look again at
     this love and lack,
wonder if this is why I leash my body, why I still try to
     root an un-rootable history, why
I worship mortal colour, why I sing & tremble in the after.

All of Us [Who?]

Sometimes I think about the phrase Arab-Israeli. A tainted beauty, a false unity when the word conflict is absent. A promise, perhaps, a threat. I think of Saud, that godless kingdom, that mad(e) house of money. Maybe I mean to say gaudy. What I know for certain is twofold: Muslims pray in one direction and Mecca exists on no map. No compass works there. This is to say that it is perfectly possible to be lost without moving a foot, without leaving the house. I reserve so much contempt for the murderous militarism of the West, but stay quiet about the cannibal Arabs who aid them in devouring the blood and bodies of our people, who grow glutton on the profit of our destruction, who open their skies to Israeli jets while some Israeli Jews choose prison in protest instead of joining their monstrous brethren, & who keep one foot on the mouths of every Palestinian and every poet. I say nothing as I haven't yet found a language for that kind of hatred, that emptiness, and I'm not sure if I should. Sometimes even a ventriloquist must fall silent
with dread for what a mouth can do.

O my lost kin, who I dream of yet have never seen, were you ever real?

Galaxies of Road

My foot is trying to communicate with the stars.
The rigid architecture of it buzzes.
I rub the hard arch, feel the harsh static heat
of distant burning. My grandmother
used to terrify my siblings and me with feet
made of bark, bigger than our bodies.
She never thought herself lost.
Her language made a country of her mouth,
it scorched the air, a whiplash snagging
ungrateful kids to work to ease her
work. I tried to knead the factory out
of her muscle, small fingers bending into
ache while she whispered och, och, och
Ya Allah, building into a chorus of praise to pain.
She was still alive, then. In the ground
she is buzzing, talking to the stars who know
what it is to have to walk so far
to be with family, to travel beyond themselves
in order to live a paler life some mistake
for fire. I don't know if I have anything to say
to those galaxies of road, the blessed realm
reserved for she who knows herself
without shame, who does not worship
suffering but accepts its burden
be it on her back or in a butcher's garden.
Whenever I think myself lost, my unworked foot
recalls hers, tunes in, a struck bell to loss &
I wait, how I wait, to hear it ring.

Meaning

for George Abraham

I am tired of summoning my heritage out of a battered magician's hat.
Yaani, there are times I reach for history and come up empty.
Yaani, it feels wrong to sing for my supper with a ghost's mouth.
Yaani, I have come to love belonging nowhere, I priest absence.
Yaani, this mo(u)rning I arranged a bouquet for my other half.
Yaani, I can multitask longing in every direction.
Yaani, when you can give directions to a stranger, you are home.
Yaani, when I planted a kiss on an Adam's apple, I entered Eden.
Yaani, I know what it is to be expelled and fear it more than anything.
Yaani, I taste the apple anyway. I am thrown every time.
Yaani, the snake has no gender. I swallow the whole pregnant length.
Yaani, to create a garden is to make a border. Even beauty is walled.
Yaani, I refuse to make ugliness a refugee. Let them stay.
Yaani, do not draw fixed lines around my origin. I came from water.
Yaani, there are waves resonating ever outward. Forget the dirt.
Yaani, meaning Arabs are forever

   transmuting tongue into ocean   to say we are here.

As the Raven Flies

I have to say it as plain as possible: I left
and have returned—the prodigal 'burb
boy, son of alleys, child of salat & haram
riding in the back of a paddy wagon no
more. I was caught only once. I thought
this meant I learned from my mistakes
but here I am, back in the house I raised
hell in, and had hell raised in me, a new
and particular shaitan, a devil I helped
father. How keen we are to lay roots
in sin. I have grown in this satin sexy,
trying to perform my way out of trauma.
It's not working. I still don't know
who I am, though I have a perfect mask,
an approximation built in the dark
to fool everyone but myself. Whatever
I learn in the world I leave in the world
for someone else to find, or a flower.
I keep only my body, somewhat wiser
but unwilling to speak of it. I look up
the word Arab and I'm unsurprised
to find it has many meanings: desert,
nomad, merchant, raven, comprehensible—
you see why I have to say things plain
now? We are so much to so many
but the least of all to ourselves. I am
home today wherever home may be,
in sear in stone in wing in speech

and yes of course in this sweet sin,
a currency I will exchange for no other.

Great Waters Keep Moving Us

for Nathaniel Tarn

I haven't seen it in years and I'm not sure
it still exists, an old man is known to say
at the beginning of every sentence.

There is a fire house out here, I mean
not where flame lives but the brigade
of its children, that is also a museum.

The story goes that over time firemen saved art
or enough of it to decorate their walls.
Now, in an emergency, you can see it too.

The river does nothing I am free
to tell you about. You should ask it
some day if it remains willing, able,

blue. The business of being a legend,
the poet knows, is simple: just fuck
up and flee the wreck to get good

enough perspective. Don't stay
home or still. You can't be rewarded
if you're never there and lack

of reward is where poetry lives.
There is a famous church here
but it is closed for the Super Bowl,

the pigeons alone do not care.
They are perched, listening above
the suffering table. Who built it,

who? My ego is too busy to answer
but I promise to take a message
and get back to them. Can't they see

I am assembling debris
from my survivable catastrophe
ready to build a legend.

Heaven Is a Bad Name

I can't imagine it, whatever it is, as a place
gated. What need the spirit for doors? What god

bothers with a wall? They who should not enter
will not enter of their own accord—grace

is poison to them. And that is only if they dared
to dream of an after. Most don't. They pray

to nothing and to nothing they will return.
This is what some of us suspect: absence

is a god, too—how could it be anything less
with so many adherents? Remaining in place

is sinful to at least one deity, I tell myself
to make leaving easier. I can't imagine it

whatever it is, as a place with a past. Anything
with a history knows pain. Nobody holy should

remember the flesh & this is proof I have never been
holy. I keep kneeling and kissing fatherhood

lightly, just the tip of it. Heaven is a bad name
for what any man can conjure, just look

at what we keep doing here, the damage
to every kind of green, every long ecstatic

tributary. We've had an eternity already to love
godhood, this elaborate glamour, this throne

covered in fluttering ladybugs & all we
did was dig graves into its sides & pour

oil into its eyes & drown children in its mouth.
I can't imagine al-Jannah, whatever it is, as a place

because then it would be real, and vulnerable.

In Order to Return

A body comes
A body goes

A religion comes
A religion goes

It would not be faith
Were it constant.

It is human
So human

To leave.

Acknowledgments

I wrote most of these poems on the lands of the Wurundjeri peoples of the Kulin Nation, and to their elders, I give thanks. I stand in solidarity with Indigenous communities around the world whose unceded lands are occupied, who continue to face injustice on their sovereign countries. Thank you to Creative Victoria and to the Australia Council for the Arts, who in 2017 and 2018, respectively, provided funding that allowed me to set aside some much-needed time to write, and to the following publications that have published twenty-six of the poems in this collection: *Prairie Schooner*, *Stilts*, *Wildness*, *Tinderbox*, *Asian American Writers' Workshop*, *Yellow Medicine Review*, *Island*, *Griffith Review*, *Ibis House*, *Meanjin*, *Peril*, *Cordite Poetry Review*, *The Big Black Thing: Chapter 2*, *Círculo de Poesía*, *Antic*, *Overland*, *Mizna*, and Melbourne's City of Literature office.

I would also like to thank WestWords and Varuna House for providing a space in which to work for a week alongside editor Elena Gomez, who provided valuable insights as I was assembling my manuscript. To my first readers, Philip J. Metres, Nathaniel Tarn, and Caitlin Maling, thank you for giving me the gift of your consideration. To my friend Lexi Alexander, without whom I could not have written "Do Not Rush," a poem near and dear to my heart, I owe a debt I'm unsure I can repay, but nevertheless I will try. To Jericho Brown and Kaveh Akbar, two poets I have written poems to, or around, in this collection: thank you for allowing me to work with your work, and thank you for your generous guiding light in general. To my brother Najwan Darwish, who remains an unswerving beacon of poetry in my world and who I will forever cherish, I have only love. To Michael Mohammed Ahmad, thank you for appreciating what no one else appreciates and blazing the way forward for literary Lebs.

In addition, I would like to acknowledge my Turkish grandmother, Yurdanur, as well as my Lebanese grandmother, Amne, and her daughter—my aunty Jamileh—who raised me, as they all have. They are my everything. I am nothing without the incredible Muslim Arab and Turkish women in my life, who have hurt and healed me, who have loved me close and loved me distant. The poems in which I refer to them are of my life, which is to say a memory or fantasy or mix of both, not their lives. They deserve more than any poem or book could hope to give them.

To my mother, the strongest and strangest person I know . . . Ya immi, what can I say? I love you more than language can encompass. Yet every time I try to hold you in my mind, I come away burned. Burning. I am trying to welcome the scalding, trying to forgive. Did you know that to forgive means to give completely? I know I have not given enough. May God grant me the courage to have this conversation in life and not just in literature.

Lastly, to any politician who picks this up: resign. Failing that, stop bombing the Middle East, stop supporting dictators, stop arming the world in the name of war and calling it peace. Lead with kindness, or not at all.

Salaam, Omar

Omar Sakr is a bisexual Arab-Australian poet. His debut collection, *These Wild Houses* (2017), was shortlisted for the Judith Wright Calanthe Award and the Kenneth Slessor Prize. His poetry has been published in English, Arabic, and Spanish in numerous journals and anthologies. He placed runner-up in the Judith Wright Poetry Prize and was the 2019 recipient of the Edward Stanley Award. Omar has performed his work nationally and internationally. He lives in Sydney.

Andrews McMeel Publishing
a division of Andrews McMeel Universal
1130 Walnut Street, Kansas City, Missouri 64106

www.andrewsmcmeel.com

The Lost Arabs was first published in Australia in 2019 by
University of Queensland Press.

20 21 22 23 24 BVG 10 9 8 7 6 5 4 3 2 1

ISBN: 978-1-5248-5401-0

Library of Congress Control Number: 2019948660

ATTENTION: SCHOOLS AND BUSINESSES
Andrews McMeel books are available at quantity discounts with bulk
purchase for educational, business, or sales promotional use. For information,
please e-mail the Andrews McMeel Publishing Special Sales Department:
specialsales@amuniversal.com.